The Extraordinary World of
The Football Fan

Being a fan is not about spectating...

it's about...

glamour

freedom

tension

excitement

doubt

togetherness

joy

solitude

Photography: Mark Leech

the experience of a lifetime in just 90 minutes...

SUPERSTITIONS

There are some supporters who go an entire season without changing their lucky pants (having washed them in the week, one hopes). Others have a compulsory meeting place or pre-match mantra. Still more dissolve in a panic if some miscreant disrupts their carefully choreographed four-hour Saturday routine. 'That's it! We'll lose now! And all because you had to buy me a bloody Bounty instead of a Snickers!'

Football superstitions are a self-imposed burden, a means of contributing to proceedings otherwise played out by manager, officials and players. We might not actually believe that whispering 'Force field' before each opposition corner averts disaster, but dare we run the risk of seeing what happens if we don't? Of course not.

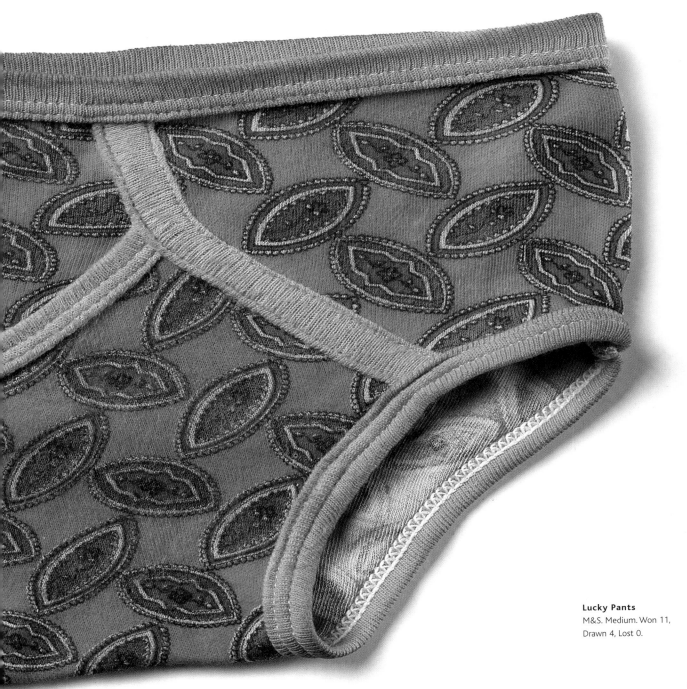

Lucky Pants
M&S. Medium. Won 11,
Drawn 4, Lost 0.

FREE SPEECH

Someone, somewhere, worked out that when 10,000 football fans roar at once it produces enough energy to boil a kettle. And presumably enough hot air is generated from the guff opinions most people vent each match to fly Richard Branson to Mars and back.

This is one of the greatest things about going to football – you can say things you can't say anywhere else. You have an audience, you have passionate views and you don't have to be eloquent. A simple 'Get that useless twat off' will suffice.

If you want to elevate yourself within the chorus line it's good to have a phrase or two that you make yours each match. Someone three rows back may already own 'On the deck lads!' but you can still monopolise 'Give and go, give and go!' or 'Make an option for him!' It is not a requirement that the phrase means anything; you are not the manager. There again, part of the shocking revelation of the *Graham Taylor: The Impossible Job* TV documentary was just how much fan-style drivel the then England manager actually spoke.

What's refreshing is that if you stay within the limits of decency you can be as illogical, biased and outspoken as you like. You can go on about how crap someone is for as long as you like – no-one really cares. It's very rare that anyone will contradict you; they'll be too wrapped up in their own version of the game to enter into debate. On the rare occasions when someone does dispute your comments, the trick is never to look the person in the face (always watch the action) and keep chipping in observations from the match that support your view. Even if you are proved absolutely wrong at the end of the game never concede defeat. Simply rise to your feet and in a self-satisfied way declare 'See, I told you so'.

REF!
THAT WAS
NEVER
A
PENALTY

SEND
HIM
OFF!
OFF!
OFF!

LISTEN TO ME

You think you are
FREE
You think you can
RUN AND PLAY
But you are wrong
You are a prisoner

ELD BY THE MAN
IN BLACK

HO ARE
ESE MEN O
HADOW ?

HO ARE
ESE MEN I
BLACK ?

04:00

BALLS

Am I so round with you as you with me,
That like a football you spurn me thus?
You spurn me hence and he will spurn me hither;
If I last in this service you must case me in leather.

From *Comedy Of Errors* by William Shakespeare

Set to a statutory circumference (68–71cm) since 1872, the football was normally mud-brown until floodlights arrived in the fifties. New-fangled balls could then be white or black-and-white or even, in the early sixties, orange – especially on snowy days. Subbuteo and other football spin-offs joined in the colour frenzy (by the way, why were Subbuteo balls all so huge, except the special ones for World Cup sets?). Then the era of marketing dawned and balls started to carry all sorts of mesmerising markings.

Though every fan can probably name their favourite ball design of yesteryear, it's always the next ball you encounter that's the most important. In fact, put virtually anything vaguely spherical in front of most fans and that seemingly humble object will take on amazing properties. Wherever you are – in the street, at work or in your bedroom – with some sort of ball at your feet you can become anyone you want, playing in any stadium you choose. While everyone admires the latest ballistic technology to come from Mitre, Nike or Adidas, even a beaten up tin can is capable of creating magic.

PREHISTORIC BALL
c.100,000,000 BC

These ancient balls were extremely durable, although they were never popular with bare-footed players.

NATURAL BALL
Ancient Greece

Players enjoyed the softness, but the ball was often quartered and eaten at half time. First ball to bounce.

MEDIEVAL BALL
c.1500s

Stuffed pig bladder balls were popular amongst rural players. Tended to smell if cradled by the keeper for too long.

LEATHER BALL
c.1900s

Round, bouncy and guaranteed to give you a headache for a week if you got on the end of a corner.

MODERN BALL
c.1990s

First ball to take on player-like
characteristics, i.e. smooth, expensive
and able to move from team to
team at great speed.

OFFICE BALL
c.1940s - Present day

Invented by bored executives in
the early Fifties. Small, but much
more fun than a calculator.

WAREHOUSE BALL
Present day

Immensely popular amongst
those who work with packaging
materials. Tendency to unfurl when
you attempt a banana shot.

UNIVERSAL BALL
Timeless

The one ball everyone has played
with. Particularly popular with the
younger generation. Makes the
best noise.

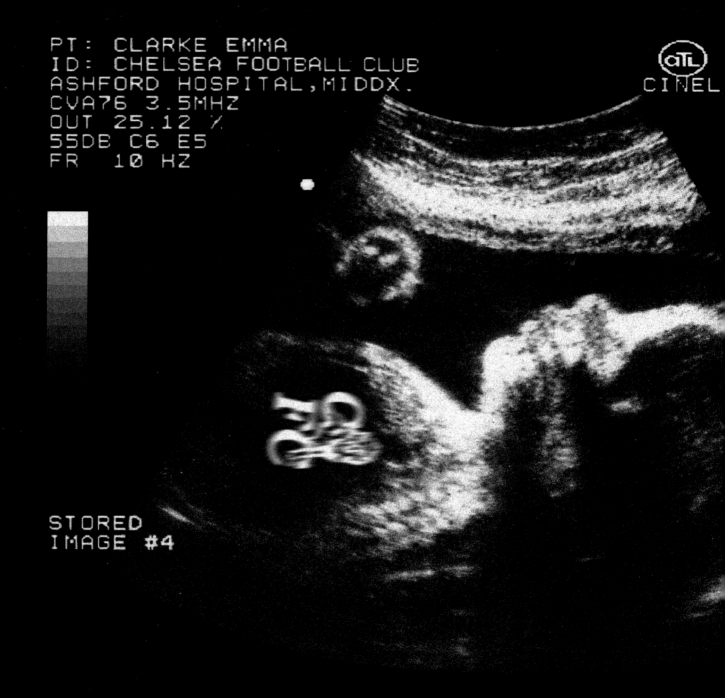

PT: CLARKE EMMA
ID: CHELSEA FOOTBALL CLUB
ASHFORD HOSPITAL,MIDDX.
CVA76 3.5MHZ
OUT 25.12 %
55DB C6 E5
FR   10 HZ

ATL
CINEL

STORED
IMAGE #4

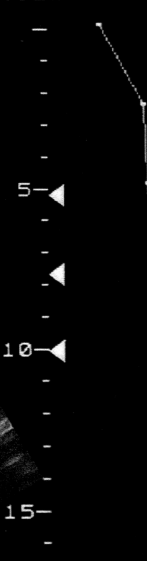

THE PARENT'S ADAGE

My child can choose their birthday presents, their favourite sweets and their computer games. They can choose their friends and their clothes. They can choose their sexuality and their god. They can choose their job, their lifestyle and their politics. They can even choose to present home decorating programmes on BBC2. But as to their football team, they have no choice
– they follow my team.

While players are now required by their clubs to adopt a more fitness-conscious, Continental-style eating regime, many of those same clubs still insist on serving up less-than-nutritious fare to their customers. Indeed, most stadium cuisine is far apart from Norwich's training ground kitchen, where director and TV chef Delia Smith insists on a pre-match sun-dried tomato risotto accompanied by feta cheese and onion bread (for the players, not the fans).

True, things are certainly changing – inside Huddersfield's excellent McAlpine Stadium, for example, you can buy a rather nice platter of chicken with salad – but a Colmans food survey of English grounds produced the unsurprising conclusion that this was still very much the exception. Wagon Wheels, Panda Pops and crisps made in Eastern Europe may all be disappearing from the game, but there are still plenty of dodgy burgers, powdered soups and unbranded chocolate bars to go around.

Of course, health issues are irrelevant when it comes down to the pie. They are a crusty institution immortalised in the 'Who ate all the pies?' chant and perpetuated in fanzine names like *Pie Muncher* (Preston) and *The Pie* (Notts County). A shop near Blackburn Rovers even used to sell 'Alan Shearer pies', although when Shearer moved on and Damien Duff broke into the team customers were not invited to try one of their 'Duff pastries' – funny that. Wherever you go in the country and despite some of the surprises that may be found inside the pastry, for many fans football simply wouldn't be football without a steaming hot pie in their hand.

Hydrolised Protein

Excreted by genetically modified pods growing in a protein farm somewhere in Lincolnshire.

Fat

Various, including industrial dripping, condensed belly fat, lard ass, and Brolin sized portions.

Chemicals

All the Es, including E150c, E211, E123, E678 (harmless), E110, E116, E402, ET, EU, EC and E I Addio (we won the cup).

Water

Source: Pond, UK.
Living organisms: 43.

**Modified
Starch**

Thickening agent, also
used in lino adhesive and
wallpaper paste. Tries to
compensate for lack of
meat content. (Fails.)

Sugar & Spice

(But nothing else nice.)

Meat

Mechanically recovered meat
from more than one dead thing.
May also contain hoof.

NEW GROUNDS

Stop all the clocks
except the sponsored ones on the big screen,
Prevent the fans from standing,
Silence the singers but pay for a hired drum,
Bring out the animal mascot,
let the corporate guests come.

Let the airship circle, moaning overhead,
Scribbling in the sky the message:
'Stadium atmosphere is dead.'

(With apologies to WH Auden)

It's a new era. When Barnsley build over the corner gap
of Oakwell where, in a dull game, the eye could follow
a stout woman walking her Rottweiler up the moor to
that last pithead in town, you know the game's up. No
more glorious, rickety grandstands resonant with history.
The old Hillsborough said it all, including why, after the
1989 disaster, football was not as important as Shanks
made out. The stadiums had to change. Or new ones
had to be built. But can you fall in love with these
new theatres of dreams?

查话朋单

查话朋单查话朋单 话朋单查话朋单 朋单查话朋单查话朋单
查查话朋单 查话朋单 查话朋单 查话朋单 查话朋单 查话朋单

Features Include:
- Confused steward figurines
- 100 restricted view seats per stand
- Speaker system
  (plays 'Simply the Best')
- Un-coordinated teenage majorette troup
- 8 burger bars
  (complete with snaking queue of fans)

Optional extras:
- Another tier
- Betting syndicate-proof floodlights
- Executive car park
- Remote coach park
- Additional action figureines,
  (including riot police)
- Away fans
- Matchday host/forgotten former player
- Nervous touts

For Chairmen of all ages !

MODEL KIT

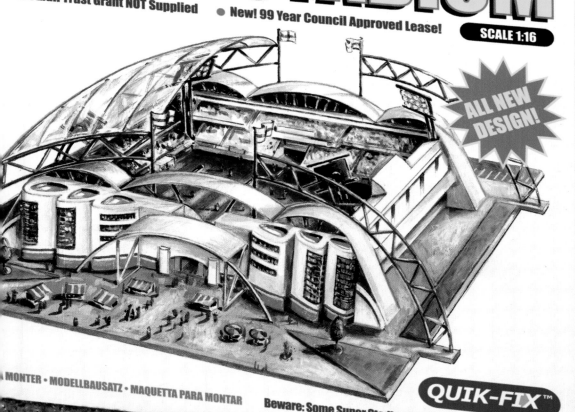

SUPER STADIUM
Football Trust Grant NOT Supplied • New! 99 Year Council Approved Lease!

QUIK-FIX™
SCALE 1:16

SUPER STADIUM

● **Football Trust Grant NOT Supplied**   ● **New! 99 Year Council Approved Lease!**

SCALE 1:16

ALL NEW DESIGN!

MONTER • MODELLBAUSATZ • MAQUETTA PARA MONTAR

QUIK-FIX™

Beware: Some Super Stadium items may stick in the throat

12:00

It was the enigmatic Gary Lineker who once suggested Wimbledon fans would enjoy football more if they watched their team on Ceefax (he might have been joking, it's difficult to tell sometimes). The truth is that no-one would actively choose to spend 90 minutes of their life in front of a screen full of ugly flickering text, but often there's no choice. In truth, the sight of someone attempting to change a pixelated 0-0 into 1-0 purely through mental determination and desperation is not pretty. And there's no emptier feeling that when you've spent an hour and a half straining, shouting and coaxing the screen to register a goal and a limp '0-0 F/T' comes up on your screen.

But as with everything to do with football, it's those golden moments of joy that keep you addicted. It's the memories of the last-minute away match winner that turned '2-2 89 mins' into '2-3 F/T'. And then there was the time your lot smashed someone 5-0 and the long list of scorers' names inspired you to take a photograph of the screen.

Apparently, the enjoyment of a thrashing on Teletext isn't limited to the fans of the victors. Connoisseur text-watchers are able to cite great moments, such as 12 September 1989, when Liverpool's scorers in a 9-0 drubbing of Crystal Palace took up a whole page of text.

Another part of the attraction is the speed with which news and rumour come up on screen. Go on to 302 or 410 and you're guaranteed some of the latest titillating transfer speculation and reports of in-club conflict to leak out from agents' offices, leaky boardrooms or disgruntled training grounds. While that's great entertainment for us, it can give those involved a bit of a shock. Just ask Harry Bassett – he discovered he was on his way from Forest when he flicked on to Teletext.

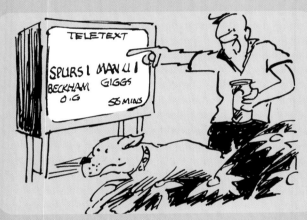

14:00

IN MY DAY

The older generation's assertion that a few Mackesons, pie and chips, bus fare, match programme, entrance to the ground, more chips, more beers and a tram home would leave you with the best part of sixpence left of a shilling was always annoyingly impressive. How refreshing it is when you realise that it's just another one of the rose-tinted lies told about Football In The Olden Days.

In their day 'there was never any violence', and yet as long ago as the turn of the century drunken fans were being blamed for attacking opposition team players in bars and running riot in the streets.

On the pitch, Stan Mortenson could 'run the length of the field not touching the ball, sending players into the stands left and right with the sheer befuddlement of his body swerves'. Oh yes? Then why does it look to the modern viewer of archive footage that the defenders were as mobile as supertankers and Stan himself was slower than the fattest linesman you've ever seen?

The fact is that football has got faster, more technical and (mostly) better year by year. You only have to watch documentaries showing the way players used to train to realise that they wouldn't stand the pace out there in a competitive match today. A few sessions with a skipping rope, a jog round the pitch and five minutes catching and throwing a medicine ball do not a Giggsy make, especially when half the teams back then seemed to exist on a diet of fish suppers and Woodbines.

When parents hand down to their children tales of the 'greats' of yesterseason they are passing on the knowledge required for a fuller appreciation of the club, but absolutely none of it is true, objective fact. To test this theory think about the players you worshipped as a kid. Look at the old photos you have and dig out some footage showing them in action. Now compare that to the athletes who hare up and down the pitch in your colours every weekend. It's not just the 'uniforms' and boots that have changed.

ZARD PHOTO. CLAPHAM

James v Giggs
How would the Arsenal captain from the 30s, Alex James, have fared against United's modern day wing-wizard, Ryan Giggs? Don't ask your grandad.

nothing wrong with the game becoming popular but you can't turn the TV on without seeing or hearing some passing reference to it.

We're not talking 'Match of the Day' here, we're talking children's television, chat shows, even those crap 'regional magazine programmes' you get after the news. All real fans know that most people on TV aren't really passionate about the game, they've just worked out that football is popular and popularity equals career success. This point is driven home every time we hear that a celebrity is our club's 'number one supporter, but doesn't get down to the ground as much as they would like'. Yeah, right. Apart from ex-players, you should mistrust the football affiliations of anyone on the small screen.

Perhaps the worst example of this is when a 'personality' regularly makes references to 'my boys' and diverts any reference to the game back to 'their' club. This phenomena is known as 'Eamonn Holmes Syndrome', and the effects on viewers include rising frustration followed by uncontrollable bouts of swearing at the TV screen.

Why not watch a nice film with football in it, instead? But then you have to suffer something even worse – actors trying to play footballers. It's difficult to enjoy a match scene when the thespians run around like under-powered Daleks. And then there's the classic close control sequence, when the skill-less feet of the actor are replaced by someone who can actually play a bit.

As our specially selected team shows, there are plenty of examples of this, although the masterpiece is, of course, *Escape to Victory*. There will never be a less believable footballing performance than Sylvester Stallone playing in goal for a team that also includes Pele, Bobby Moore and Alan Mullery (well, the first two anyway).

Lu

2
CAINE
(ESCAPE TO VICTORY)

6
BADDIEL
(FANTASY FOOTBALL LEAGUE)

COACH: CHERIE

① STALLONE
(ESCAPE TO VICTORY)

⑤ GLOVER
(KES)

④ BENNY
(GRANGE HILL)

③ GILMORE
(CUP FEVER)

⑦ BERRY
(EASTENDERS)

⑧ THOSE KIDS
(BEDKNOBS AND BROOMSTICKS)

⑪ HEPBURN
(GREGORY'S GIRL)

⑨ BEAN
(WHEN SATURDAY COMES)

⑩ McSHANE
(YESTERDAY'S HERO)

...GHI (THE MANAGERESS)

Who do they think they're kidding? Why don't managers and players just say what they mean? 'The ref's been a bit harsh there' – the bloke in black was bang out of order! 'We would hope he'd hit the target from that range' – the lad's had a 'mare up front. 'There's everything to play for still' – we're going down but I can't admit it yet because I'll get the sack.

No-one believes them when they come out with these vague, elusive sentences. We would all give them much more respect if they simply said what they thought. But of course, managers and players are now coached in how to handle their number one enemy – the media – and that's partly what leads them to talk such rubbish. This is clearly wrong, and we long for the day when, for example, an England manager has the guts to say 'You know, I would love it, really love it, if we stuffed Germany on penalties.' But for now, well, if you want the truth you just have to read between the lines.

"We're pleased

We fouled them and

~~with our commit~~

~~incident.~~ [I woul

our players, bu

skipper played

put a price on

We spent 90 minutes

manager why the

~~keeper's made s~~

sometimes you re

through, but you

Chairman –

~~squad they have~~

h the result. ~~I was happy~~ *~~away with it~~*

t. ~~I didn't see the handball~~
, *It was definitely a penalty* →

't like to single out one of

f you look at the way our

the park today you couldn't
— ANY OFFERS ??

]. ~~You'll have to ask their~~
ing to work out their formation
~~ined up the way they did.~~ Our

~~world class saves out there,~~
ur defence was non-existent
on your quality to win

~~ave to look at the depth of~~
g into your pockets or I'm off !!

20:00

SCARVES

Will they ever be back in vogue? In the seventies youngsters couldn't get enough of them: silk ones, woolly ones; team colours, tartans; round the waist, round the head, round the wrist. Shapeless ones Gran knitted where the blue or the red or the green wasn't quite right. Machined ones bought from a stall with 'Division Two Runners-up 1981' mis-spelt, twice.

Today, they're often discreetly tucked under a jacket, a tasteful flash of adherence. But on the motorway you can see them flying from a closed window, flapping in the breeze like standards going into battle (and often lost when the passenger seeks ventilation).

To a great extent the scarf has been replaced by the replica shirt, but there are advantages to the scarf, not least the fact that if you ever come across a gang of opposing supporters in a backstreet you can always untie it from whatever body part it is attached and chuck it over the nearest wall. Doing this with a £39.99 replica shirt tends to attract more attention and is economically painful.

However, shirts dominate and in England particularly we've largely forgotten the emotive power of scarves deployed in unison. Only the Scots have perservered, and even then it's only on very special occasions. Over on the Continent the simultaneous swirling of several thousand bits of wool still stirs the soul on a regular basis, and in Eastern Europe you'll see displays of colour that put us to shame. Perhaps the domestic game needs some foreign imports in the stands to bring back the heyday of the scarf?

Rumours fulfil a deep-seated need in the football fan to be misled pleasurably. That they are perpetrated by tabloid hacks with little more insight than the average PE teacher is neither here nor there.

Close season is the dream time, when empty columns scream out to be filled by any old hogwash. This is when the real fantasy football happens, with all sorts of superstars 'definitely' on their way to you, or your despised neighbours, or Real Madrid. Of course, the main principle here is to enjoy all the uncertainty, the amazing possibilities and the conjecture, and then only believe what you want to.

Ronaldo on his way to us, supposedly

by Sarah's mate Tony

ACCORDING to a bloke I met through work (only turns out he's a season ticket holder and lives next door to that Radio 5 Live woman, doesn't it). Ronaldo was spotted getting out of a limo outside our ground last week.

Makes you think. We could never afford his bloody wage bill but what was he doing there? Apparently his wife has been looking round local estate agents too.

Another class

It makes sense though. We definitely need a bit more class up front. Not sure how well he would work alongside Woodsy – well they thrive off

a different sort of ball, don't they. But you could see him making a difference in those key games.

Lord Nelson

Not sure whether he has any kids, but no doubt his wife has been looking round the schools. I reckon he would love it here, even if it is a bit cold in January. He'll love it, especially with that new Asda on the ring road. I'm going to ask Lenny what he knows. He did the roof on the training ground changing rooms last year and he says he's right in with Pottsy the physio now. They drink down the Nelson on Wednesdays. Maybe Ronaldo was in there last week?

'Top Italian striker is definitely gay' – reckons London cabbie

From his fare

A TAXI DRIVER taking me home from a boozy leaving do the other week dropped a bombshell that will shake football to its foundations. He says a few weeks earlier he'd picked up that Italian forward with another fella and took them back to his place.

Own Eyes

"If I hadn't seen it with my own eyes I would never have believed it," the cab driver said. "It was him all right - I recognised him from Goal of the Month on the box. Funny eyes. All over the other bloke like a cheap suit. They're like that over there – remember the Romans? And the wages they get".

Disgrace

"You'd think they'd keep it to themselves, wouldn't you?" said the cabbie. "It's no better on the pitch. You've seen them when they score – kissing and hugging. Disgusting I call it. Unnatural. You didn't see Billy Bremner or Tommy Smith doing that sort of thing. A brief handshake was pushing it. They should leave their foreign ways at home. It's a man's game over here."

LEAGUE ROUND UP
Our club has 'got loads of money really'

A group of drunken supporters
Reporting from the pub

WHERE does the money go? That's the question being asked by at least three people who have just seen their team lose another game because the players aren't good enough and the squad needs additions to the gene pool.

Totally loaded

They keep telling us they haven't got any money to buy players, but Colin, who's basically the only one of us who can count, has worked out that an average gate of 13,500 for every home game over the last three seasons at something like £10 per ticket works out to... well, I can't remember the actual figure but it was quite a lot and we're not seeing any of that being spent on bloody players are we?

Continued column 4, page 36

WILSON AND JONES SHOCK: THEY HATE EACH OTHERS GUTS!

According to this geezer

WHAT I'VE HEARD, right, is that they clashed in pre-season when the team went away to that training camp in Portugal. The defender was chatting up one of the waitresses when his wife rang on the mobile that was lying on the table. Wilson, who was supposed to be a bit

the worse for wear, picked up the phone and said something like "He can't talk now love, he's trying to get his leg over".

Big tackle

Anyway, that obviously caused some bad blood and the first chance he got Jones went in with

a crunching challenge and 'did' him. That's why he missed the first few matches of the season, but it's all been hushed up. Now they don't even talk to each other. I've been told that Coventry are in for one of them now, but which one escapes us at the moment.

CITY AND UNITED TO SHARE GROUND!

NO, HEAR ME OUT! I met the City masseur while I was on holiday in Florida — bloody nice bloke actually.

One night I got to talk to him for ages about the players and the club and, straight up, he said that we were

Demi Moore to open new Superstadium

going to share the new United stadium. He sounded like he was joking at first, but the more drinks we had the more he went on about it.

Thick

He reckons the directors at City and United only pretend to hate each other. Apparently they're thick as thieves.

The City stadium is going to be demolished and turned into a multiplex cinema. They reckon that Demi Moore is going to fly over and open it.

FULL STORY: PAGE 47

I LENT SHEARER A FIVER!
Full story inside

24:00

KIT SPONSORS

Today every half-decent player is a moving billboard for someone or something, it seems. For the away-day traveller the kit sponsors' page in the programme is the bit you reach after four hours of a five hour journey, but it's often worth sifting through for the odd gem of unglamorous association. There are portly outfield players whose benefactors are breweries or pie shops and leaky goalkeepers with local plumbers to their name. Then there are the pros who simply can't attract any sponsors at all. You can't blame the sponsors really – the player's unlikely to be as cute as other deserving causes, like an animal in the local zoo, and there is never an open day where they get to meet the socks they have financed for the last nine months.

As a sponsor, you generally don't get that much for your money. Despite this, new and peculiarly appropriate financiers keep coming out of the woodwork. For example, in 1997-98 Wayne Brown, a centre-half, played just one game for Ipswich: the people coughing up for his kit were – and this is completely true – a company called 'Find A Job'. The same season, slap-headed Ray Wilkins' Crystal Palace togs were paid for by 'Galv's Hair Studio'. And in 1998-99 the sponsor of about-to-leave West Ham player Eyal Berkovic was the shop 'Bygones'. But what of the fans' reactions to the names emblazoned across their own prized replica kit? What, for example, was the response of Upton Park's Cockney rhyming slang faithful when the Hammers took the money from shirt manufacturers Pony? To a commercial department it's just the highest bidder; to the fan it could be the difference between pride and humiliation. No supporter would be happy, for example, if moneyed Czech medical firm Wank stepped in with a multi-million pound deal to smear their name over the team's chests.

A **Bootlaces**

New OPPORTUNITY

39503/BL	8 EYELETS	BLACK

Your name or business in white
Maximum of 16 characters

● 1 season deal £149.99
● 3 season deal £349.99

26:00

He turns up to the ground and no one asks for his autograph. No one shouts out his name. But once he's put on a synthetic animal outfit and adopted his trademark funny walk, suddenly... he's mobbed by kids, sung to from the stands and hugged by players – he's a star! But just who are the people inside the costumes (they can't all be the brother-in-law of the half-time DJ)? And what do they do when they're not at the football? It remains a mystery.

Unfortunately, some of our furry friends are now beginning to mimic the antics of players. Indeed, these child-charmers lost their innocence forever in 1998, when Bristol City met visitors Wolverhampton Wanderers. City had invited some 'Little Pigs' from a local double glazing firm to accompany their usual 'City Cat' mascot. Wolves arrived with their now traditional 'Wolfie' character. The Wolves beast, revelling in his team's 2-1 lead, ran towards the Wanderers end, arms aloft. However, he was intercepted en route and cuffed by one of the pigs, who was swiftly followed into the comic mêlée by the other fancy dress porcines and 'City Cat', who, as a wearer of oversize spectacles, should have known better. Eventually the mascots were separated, but as the teams emerged for the second half the wolf sneakily landed a left paw and the whole thing went off again.

A few months later nine-foot-tall 'Cyril The Swan' was banned from the Swansea touchline after running on to the pitch in celebration of a City goal against Millwall. In an unrelated incident, Bolton's 'Lofty The Lion' had meat pies thrown at him. It seems some of our cuddly heroes are endangered species.

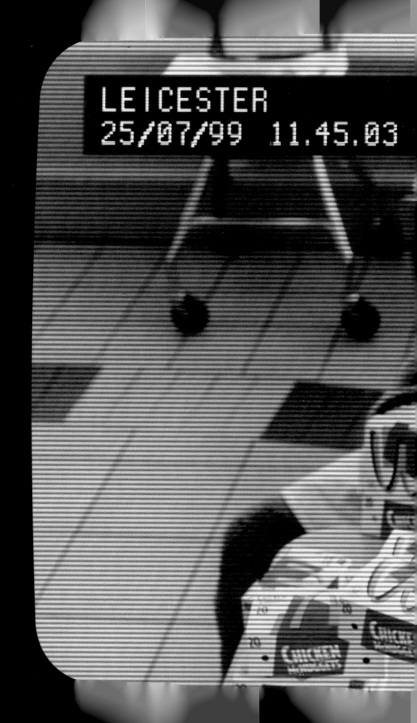

LEICESTER
25/07/99 11.45.03

A mascot's day off
Even Leicester City's 'Filbert Fox' has to rest sometimes. Here he's spotted snacking on his favourite food.

FIG. 1: THE WRISTY

Implication that the opposition supporters or players enjoy indulging in sexual pleasure whilst they are alone.

FIG. 2: THE RULER

The attempt on goal achieved a less than desirable result, missing the designated target area by an amount indicated by the distance between the hands. Often accompanied with a shrill 'arghhhhhhhhhh'.

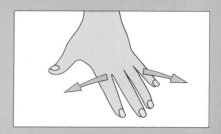

FIG. 3: THE SHAKY

The opposition goalkeeper has demonstrated behaviour that suggests he is likely to under-perform in his role as custodian of the goal. Most often witnessed at corners, goal kicks and matches featuring Scottish keepers.

SIGN LANGUAGE

Supporters don't let distance or the limitations of the chanted word hold them back from communicating with their opposition counterparts. Indeed, an entire non-verbal language takes place during a game, with each side keen to ensure that the others know exactly where they stand on all of the key issues of the day. How nice.

FIG. 4: THE AIRPLANE

Depending on context; aeronautical accidents have not been kind to the opposition club's personnel; opposition player has a fear of aeronautical travel; opposition player is German.

FIG. 5: THE WAVE

Most often seen in the final minutes of a game as one set of supporters wishes the other farewell. Fans appear particularly keen to adopt this when their team has soundly beaten the opposition and rival fans are attempting to leave quietly before the full 90 minutes have been completed.

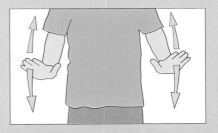

FIG. 6: THE CALMER

Suggestion that opposition fans may be wise to relax, regain their composure and generally reach a state of calm after outburst of passion. This advice often offered to supporters hailing from the north-west of England.

ARMCHAIR FANS

There's so much football on TV now that everyone has become an armchair fan to some extent. The crucial difference is whether you change your viewing patterns when your team is playing or whether you stay firmly wedged into the furniture.

Watching a game in the relative comfort of your home does have some advantages. You get a great view and you can drink alcohol in your seat. And for those with a short attention span there are always action replays and pundits showing you what really happened by drawing on the screen.

So, OK, there's comfort and ease and funny little arrows, but don't kid yourself that you're getting the most from the game. You're missing everything from the nattering in the pub to the wonderfully smelly and exciting walk to the ground; from singing as loud as you can to a view of the action away from the ball (like your left back having a quick dig at someone when the ref isn't watching). And since when has anyone managed to wind up an entire stand full of rival fans while sitting in front of their telly?

Basically, stay at home and you're missing a wonderful sensory overload. Football is a game best experienced live and raw, and by every single one of your senses at the same time. That's why the armchair should never be the preferred option.

Having said that, in this era of grounds sold out to season ticket holders and admission prices getting silly, we shouldn't be too sniffy about TV. How else can thousands of fans of bigger clubs get to see their heroes play? Well, clearly something is needed to improve the lives of all those unfortunate armchair fans who would really (honestly) rather be there at the ground. Something like the cards shown here; you'd simply scratch away to fill your own home with the authentic aroma of pre-match pub, crowd and stadium.

HALF-TIME SCRATCH

Queueing

Quick Slash

B.O.

Instructions: 1.Scratch gently with a coin. 2.Waft card around a bit.

POST-MATCH SCRATCH

Your Clothes

Same again

Success
(Sweet smell)

Instructions: 1.Scratch gently with a coin. 2.Waft card around a bit.

OTBALL

CH

e deposits

ound a bit.

WHATEVER IT TAKES

What would you do to ensure you saw your team in a final, a league decider or your most important local derby? The problem is obvious; the game you most want to see is always the game that's hardest to get into. But very little stands in the way of a hardcore fan who's absolutely determined to be there.

When a team attracts a lot of passionate support something has to give, and it often used to be a side door or a bit of vulnerable fencing. Indeed, big away mobs used to push in gates to gain access with great regularity. What was the 'White Horse Final' – the 1923 FA Cup final – if it wasn't a demonstration of 250,000 fans' burning desire to see the two teams, Bolton and West Ham, and their contempt for the brand new Wembley Stadium's security?

Until recently there were still a whole host of ways the talented could push, blag or ghost their way into a ground. Each year one individual used to make imaginative use of the away end toilets at The Dell at Southampton. Arriving early in the morning on match day, he would wait in his locked cubicle until the crowds started rolling in and he could emerge from his hideout looking suitably refreshed (hello Chris if you're reading).

It all seemed a bit of a laugh. But then there was the horror of Hillsborough, and suddenly all the dodgy fences, climbable walls and bad policing up and down the country stopped looking like golden opportunities to get in and more like another disaster waiting to happen.

Today stadia are built better, security is tighter and safety is thought about more carefully, just as it should have been from the start. But the mass of passion and desire to get in, whatever it takes, lives on – and what gives now is usually the desperate fan's bank balance so they can buy from a tout.

But that's nothing. For some ex-pats, attending a game costs more than a tout makes on a good night at Old Trafford. And even when someone has the money, the trip doesn't always go to plan. Take the story of the Geordie supporter living in America. It was 1993 and he was ecstatic that his club were likely to be promoted back to the top flight. He looked up the fixture list for May to see that his beloved Mags were playing the potential clincher against Oxford in midweek. So he quit his job, spent his savings on the flight home, caught a taxi to Oxford from Heathrow and arrived at the Manor Ground just in time for the evening kick-off. Unfortunately, he was 200 miles away from the glorious game, which was played at St James' Park.

MERCHANDISE

Brands are everything in today's society. Clubs were initially slow to realise this; for many merchandising meant banging out replica kits, some plastic pennants and a few key rings for the dusty stadium shop. Now, as if to make up for lost time, they're attempting to stamp the mark of the club on to everything that moves (and in some cases literally, with branded cars and motorbikes now available).

Indeed, it's amazing how far some of them will go. Worldwide brands like Nike and Coca Cola would think twice before expanding into motor insurance, hotels or wine, but many of the bigger clubs think they can make anything a success simply by attaching their name to it. Why? Because when buying normal brands people are a pretty discerning bunch, but when buying from their club they're far more influenced by emotions.

Whether buying from your club is loyalty or stupidity depends on how the profits from the sales are used and the quality of what you get back. Most fans hope that their money gets put into the war chest for transfers, but that's not always the case. It would certainly be good to see some profits go towards making facilities better at grounds, but that's not always the way it is either.

Still, the clubs are introducing more new ideas, even though a lot of questions about fans' long term loyalty as customers remain. For example, just how much of our life and how many of our possessions do we want to be related to our football club? And will we still want the club connection as much when the team's playing badly?

It's easy to be cynical about these commercial activities, but ultimately – when it comes to business at least – it's fans who have the final say. The club may have the right to use the team you love for all its commercial worth, but you and your fellow fans have the power to decide when enough is enough.

MUFC
******METRO******
OLD TRAFFORD BRANCH

	£
TEDDY SHERRY	
ANDY COLA	7.99
NICKY - I CAN'T BELIEVE	1.19
ITS NOT - BUTTER	
RYAN CHEST WIGGS	.79
DWIGHT YORKIE BAR	9.95
VESPA BLOMQVIST	.49
	1599.00

TOTAL

TOTAL   £ 1619.41

CASH   1620.00
CHANGE   .59

LEAGUE POINTS THIS VISIT   3

NEXT MATCH: v CHELSEA PLC
This is not a match ticket

******THANK-YOU******
UP THE REDS

Why not try our Smokey
Beckham crisps?

5/08/99   19:37 1012930 5678

36:00

SIGN OF THE TIMES

There you are, walking into the ground, full of the joys of the world. The team's doing alright, there's a good turn-out and you're looking forward to an entertaining game. Then you catch sight of those warning signs and you're reminded once more that, despite having paid hundreds of pounds for tickets in the past few months, you are – apparently – nothing more than a criminally-minded yob intent on causing mayhem. Yes, it's you they're talking to.

No wonder clubs have found it difficult to attract families and women into grounds – judging by the signs outside they must think they'd be walking into a war zone. The truth is that inside most stadia you're more likely to be ejected by an uptight steward for eating a homemade sandwich than you are to experience physical bother from other fans. No wonder rattles have disappeared from the stands – they'd be considered a dangerous weapon today. Where will it end? Will singing be banned for fear that it upsets visiting supporters?

At bigger grounds there's no escaping the regulations. Video cameras and stewards now watch our every move. Better security has some benefits, like weeding out the truly dangerous, but it's certainly dampened the atmosphere too. So maybe now, instead of trying to hold people back, the signs outside grounds should be attempting to get the crowd as excited and passionate as they once were.

Prohibited

The directors and stewards of the club remind fans that the following behaviour is prohibited in the ground for the safety of all users.

Carrying weapons

Standing during play

Throwing projectiles

Singing

Getting over excited

Pitch invasions

Streaking

Heated debates

Eating, drinking and being merry

By order of the management

38:00

FOOTBALL BOOKS

Writers write and footballers play football. It's as simple as that, Des. And yet, since footballers are celebrities, their autobiographies are as highly treasured as those of complex villains, world leaders and even TV chefs. The point is that fans are so desperate for insight in a game filled with platitudes that they'll buy on the off-chance that something interesting or controversial has slipped in.

Alan Shearer's *Diary of a Season*, for example, carried nothing more captivating than an exposé of the parking arrangements at Blackburn's training ground. Its context was their Championship season and all he could reveal was where Flowers preferred to leave the Range Rover. He didn't need a ghost writer so much as a poltergeist.

Of course, there have been some celebrated opuses down the years. What about Len Shackleton, with his infamous blank page representing 'what the average club chairman knows about football'. And League journeyman Garry Nelson, whose *Left Foot Forward* is a genuinely eye-opening read about the stark realities of playing in the lower divisions. But writing about football is best left to the professionals: Hugh McIlvanney, Brian Glanville, even the overrated but still salient Nick Hornby. It may be, as the old maxim goes, that 'those who can't, write about it'. The reverse is also true: those who can, can't write.

Sign of trouble
For many the Union flag was a proud emblem until it was hijacked by right wing 'fans'.

HOOLIGANS

There is no doubt that the tragedy of Heysel crystallised public enmity towards soccer yobs. But if it was the obnoxious, illiterate football tribes who drove the nice people away from football why do so many books on hooliganism shift off the shelves so fast?

It's because thousands of people who would never dream of fighting at a match remain fascinated by crowd-related violence. It's not a new phenomenon. Just a few years before Heysel the *News of the World* was publishing a weekly league table glamorising the most active 'firms'.

More recently society has allowed football to 'come home', but just as that happened so John King's *Football Factory* and *Headhunters*, Colin Ward's *Steaming In* and Bill Buford's *Among The Thugs* (along with many other hoolibooks) started to appear amongst British football's top-ten bestsellers. The fascination continues.

According to Buford, who edited the literary journal *Granta*, we shouldn't be surprised by this. 'The crowd is in all of us,' he says. 'It isn't an instinct or a need... but, for most of us, the crowd holds out certain essential attractions. It is, like an appetite, something in which dark satisfactions can be found.'

Buford adds some insight to the area, but many of the sociologists who have descended on football en masse (often attracted by the same glamour as the buyers of the books) have created some ludicrous conclusions about modern Britain on the basis of their 'readings' of football-related violence. They often seem unable to take in the simple point that, for many, 'hooligan' experiences were 99% harmless pantomime and 1% real aggression.

Where we may need the sociologists is on understanding the darkest side of all – racism and racist violence in and around football. We've certainly come some way since the eighties, when copies of *Bulldog* – the National Front's vile, mad magazine – was sold outside the nation's stadiums. But for many, the far right's adoption of the Union flag as a symbol of racial purity has sullied the emblem forever, particularly at football. Even wearing the legendary 'Union Jack' boxer shorts at overseas matches became a political choice, a nationalist statement.

Some honest, patriotic supporters still wave the red, white and blue at matches and it should stir up pride in every fan. Unfortunately, we have to share a symbol with people who have taken the flag and made it mean something most people hate.

A GAME OF TWO HALVES

Those venturing into the realms of pre-match drinking should be aware that this is an activity fraught with social niceties and anthropological bizarreness (not to mention a large dose of nerves). Yes, those people wearing brightly coloured shirts and laughing a lot might look like they're completely relaxed, but they're all players in an elaborate game. If you still want a drink you need to learn the rules.

1. *Arrange to meet early. Turn up late.*

2. *Don't discuss anything meaningful or personal, just football.*

3. *Be consistent in your views. Remember, last week you thought your left-back was world class and should be playing for his country (San Marino), so don't now say 'he's a load of rubbish and we need to sell him as fast as possible'.*

4. *Allow people to believe things about you. For example, that you know loads of the players personally; that you were there in '73; that you have inside knowledge of the chairman's plans.*

5. *Always get your round in – last (the get-there-early crowd will have left already).*

6. *Never wait for Mr Plenty-Of-Time-Yet – he always misses the kick-off.*

If you think pre-match drinking is complex wait until you experience a pub after the game. The match changes the mood, so the nervous banter and chat and laughter might have transformed into anything from wild celebration to silence. It's completely unpredictable. That's the real reason it's called a game of two halves.

TOILETS

From the corrugated troughs you find up and down the country to the unlamented old porcelain paddling pools at Wembley, something goes wrong when it comes to planning the stadium khazi. Everyone knows the problem: having once missed one of the greatest goals ever scored by their team because they were relieving themselves, every fan now waits until the last possible moment before nipping down to the facilities. When you get in there it's like a scene from hell, with crazed people crushed up against each other and performing their ablutions in all manner of vessels (basin, bin, pocket).

Things were worse before stadium redevelopments. At least in an all-seater ground your pocket is less likely to be used as a urinal. But instead of that you get queues longer than a Pat Jennings clearance. It makes you wonder why, despite having paid good money for your ticket, you have to endure such horrendous facilities. Is it that the combined brains of the world's architects have simply been unable to come up with a solution to football fans' lavatorial habits? Or is it simply that the club is taking the piss?

48:00

FOOTBALL ARGUMENTS

The key with football arguments is to never make the mistake of trying to be reasonable. If necessary, follow the logic of your argument to tortuous ends, even if you have to resort to making wild and absurd claims. Some pretty bizarre things happen in football, so if you declare that Matthew Le Tissier is wasted up front and should really be played as a centre-back, people will actually contemplate what you're saying for at least 10 seconds. By the time they've worked out that you're talking utter nonsense you'll have put together a whole new angle of attack.

Many of these arguments start out with the most high-minded intentions, but you often find it's not long before an informed discussion of the pros and cons of the Italian *catenaccio* system turns into a bout of playground shouting. The difference with school days is that 'sportsman's bets' have been replaced with real money gambles, which can be expensive if after five pints you feel inclined to make all sorts of outrageous claims for your team and your favourite players.

Even if you lose your bet, however, you can console yourself with the knowledge that both the professionals and the highly paid pundits get it wrong sometimes. Badly wrong. Just think 'You'll never win anything with kids' and 'Owen's not a natural goalscorer' and you'll feel OK again.

The newspapers talk about today's stars – the high-earning, goal-scoring, cap-winning, Ferrari-driving heroes. Fans, on the other hand, spend much more time talking about the bungling clowns of yesteryear, the huffing-puffing lumps of lard who played with two left feet and one eye.

EU Johnny Foreigner

Age:	According to agent, 20
Height:	Greek God
Weight:	Italian Stallion
Caps:	Armani, Gucci, Hugo Boss...
Goals:	To be first football billionaire (ecus)
Position:	On top
Honours:	Banking with Coutts

D Rolland Fallover

Age:	Post Italia '90
Height:	5'8" but under 2' when poleaxed
Weight:	...the harder they fall
Caps:	4 gold teeth
Goals:	To do a Triple Salko in open play
Position:	On the ground in agony
Honours:	Strictly without honour

ENG Don Key

Age:	Not allowed in pubs
Height:	Bean pole
Weight:	8 stone wringing wet
Caps:	1 (England 'B' International)
Goals:	4 (o.g.)
Position:	Bench
Honours:	Roomed with England Physio

ENG

IRE

Dear O'Dear

Age:	Been around a bit
Height:	Of fashion in the 70s
Weight:	15st 8lbs
Caps:	Sent home from training camp
Goals:	Always hit the bar
Position:	Pint in each hand
Honours:	Knew Ron Atkinson's jeweller

Gaffer

Age:	As old as he feels
Height:	Of bad taste
Weight:	Tweed
Caps:	Managerial heavyweight
Goals:	To be interviewed by Parky
Position:	In bed with the coach's wife
Honours:	18 handicap at La Manga

SCO Spilly McMuckitup

Age:	47
Height:	7' 7"
Weight:	Way, way over
Caps:	Only when the sun's in his eyes
Goals:	To be more confident at corners
Position:	Rooted to the goal line
Honours:	Dropped Leyland Duff trophy

52:00

SINGING

Take a non-fan to a game and the one thing that's bound to mystify them is the singing and chanting. Who creates the songs? How does everyone know when to sing? What are the words? Why do you all clap at the end of that line? To you all this is second nature; to the non-fan it's bizarre but fascinating behaviour. The annoying thing is that, naive though those questions sound, they're not that easy to answer.

Just who did decide to introduce *Guantanamera* to football, for example? Just why do your lot sing the same song at the same time every away game? And why is it that the bloke in front of you tries and fails to start chants every game, but the bloke behind you only has to utter half a consonant and the whole stand is in full voice?

The truth is, it feels a bit odd talking about singing. It just happens. It's unplanned. It's instinctive. And the only way the non-fan will start to get real answers to those questions is by going to more and more matches — at some point they'll be feeling the impulse just like everybody else.

○

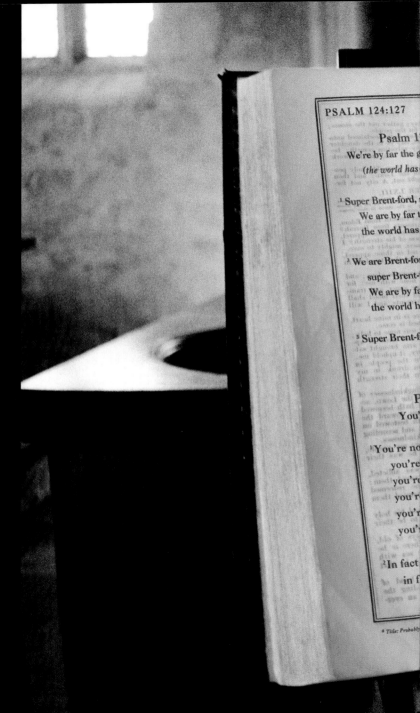

PSALM 124:127

Psalm 1
We're by far the g
(*the world has*

1 Super Brent-ford,
We are by far t
the world has

3 We are Brent-fo
super Brent-
We are by fa
the world h

5 Super Brent-f

P
You'

1 You're no
you're
you're
you'r
you'
you',

2 In fact
in f

o Title: Probably

Psalm 126

Who ate all the pies?

(Feast of Stephen)

1 Who ate all the pies?
  Who ate all the pies?
2 You fat individual
  born out of wedlock,
3 You fat individual
  born out of wedlock,
4 you ate all the pies.
                    amen.

Psalm 127

No-one likes us *(we don't care)*

1 We are Mill-wall, we are Mill-wall,
  we are Mill-wall of the den.
2 We are Mill-wall, super Mill-wall
  super Mill-wall, of the den.

3 No-one likes us, no-one likes us,
  no-one likes us, we don't care.
4 We are Mill-wall, super Mill-wall,
  we are Mill-wall, of the den.

5 We are Mill-wall, we are Mill-wall,
  we are Mill-wall of the den.
6 We are Mill-wall, super Mill-wall
  super Mill-wall, of the den.
                    amen.

7 No-one likes us, no-one likes us,
  no-one likes us, we don't care.
8 We are Mill-wall, super Mill-wall,
  we are Mill-wall, of the den.

9 We are Mill-wall, we are Mill-wall,
  we are Mill-wall of the den.
10 We are Mill-wall, super Mill-wall
  super Mill-wall, of the den.
                    amen.

Psalm 128

Ariseth if you hate Man U

(words: trad)

1 Stand up,
  if you hate Man U.
2 Stand up,
  if you hate Man U.
3 Stand up,
  if you hate Man U.
4 Stand up,
  if you hate Man U.
5 Stand up,
  if you hate Man U.
6 Stand up,
  if you hate Man U.
(clap hands)
                    amen.

Psalm 129

He's the best by far

1 Some talk about Cruyff,
2 some talk about Pele,
3 some talk about Beckenbauer,
4 But Jamie Bates,
  he's the best by far.
5 He's Batesie, Batesie,
  Jamie, Jamie Batesie,
  He's the best by far.
6 He's Batesie, Batesie,
  Jamie, Jamie Batesie,
  He's the best by far.
7 He's Batesie, Batesie,
  Jamie, Jamie Batesie,
  He's the best by far.
                    amen.

Psalm 130

And Leeds

1 We all hate Leeds
  and Leeds and Leeds
2 Leeds and Leeds
  and Leeds and Leeds.
3 We all hate Leeds
  and Leeds and Leeds
  We all

It's not just a case of betting on a result, these days you can stick money on everything from the number of times a trainer comes on to the pitch; or the off-side decisions made in the second half; or the chances of your midfield maestro's left sock falling down.

Betting can give you much-needed entertainment during a dull game, but it also skews your view of a player or a match. Imagine, your lads are 1-0 up with five minutes to go but you've got £100 riding on the other lot to get 10 corners. They lay siege to your goal and win their seventh corner, followed by another and another. Do you punch the air while all around are biting their lips... and explain your deviant actions on the way home?

56:00

RIVALRY

When Sunderland allowed fans to buy bricks with their name on it for their new Stadium of Light it wasn't long before their Tyneside rivals saw the potential for some long-standing jokes. And so anagrams of 'Newcastle United' are amongst those of the genuine founders. That's rivalry expressed as wit, but more often it comes out in an irrational form.

Take colour blindness. In Liverpool, where the red/blue divide is enforced with almost biblical fervour, Everton received abusive complaints about the colour of the new season ticket wallet. The wallets were maroon. Celtic will never have a trace of blue on their kit; Rangers feel the same way about green. (These are not laughing matters but serious social issues.) And it happens with brands too. Tottenham fans struggle to resist the allure of Nike, shirt makers for Arsenal.

There are plenty of reasons for rivalries to form, from on-field controversies to off-field jealousies, but geography is often key. Leeds Utd despise their Manchester namesakes; Norwich and Ipswich is tense; Cardiff and Swansea unpleasant; Watford and Luton Town ugly; and everyone dislikes Birmingham. The list goes on.

Take Southampton and Portsmouth. Pompey fans chime on about 'Saints scummers'. Saints, intriguingly, reply with 'Pompey skaters'. This abuse has its origins in the ports' naval histories – Southampton being merchant, Portsmouth royal navy. The Queen's sailors, it seems, spent longer at sea without a woman's company, and would improvise with flatfish, like skate.

But no-one does rivalry like the Central Americans. Take the 1970 World Cup matches between Honduras and El Salvador. The meetings were so bad tempered that the war which broke out between the two later that year was blamed on the games. It was even dubbed 'la guerra del fútbol' – The Football War.

BLOKE BEHIND YOU

You've got your ticket, you've got yourself to the ground and you've braved the snarling Alsatians. You've even fought off the temptation to buy a Cup-a-Soup from the 'café'.

You're now ready to discover what hand you have been dealt in the great game of Bloke Behind You. Just whose vocal chords will be within a few feet of your ear drums for the next hour and a half? Will it be the resident wit, full of insight and wryly observed comment? Or a bellowing lunatic whose indecipherable outbursts are accompanied by a downpour of phlegm and half-eaten pie?

The lottery is even greater for the season ticket holder. They have to sit in front of whoever it is for nine months. There lies a great dilemma: do you stay in the same seat, with its grand view and memories of past goals (particularly that celebration when your glasses flew up in the air and were found three rows in front)? Or do you get away from Charlie Boy behind you, with his old cabbage-breath, stream of moronic comments and tuneless chants?

Naturally, not every Bloke Behind You is like that. Indeed, some of football's greatest moments are produced by the timely witticisms of those unidentified football characters somewhere in the stands. And besides, though you might not have thought about it like this, to someone somewhere you're the 'Bloke Behind Me'.

10

12

11

9

8   6

7

5

3   4

2

1

◄ **You are here**

rity of football has brought
o grounds up and down the
e now hosts people experiencing
ur first game can be the most
an be like a nightmare, with
g and saying things that make
it is, you'll never forget it.

be bad for the football
rse for the regular. You bring
that they want to talk about
loud voice, look the wrong
the style of play of the
e wrong time and keep asking
ong are. You want to be free
r everyday life and immerse
ordinary world; they insist
or what they did last Tuesday.
to shut up for 45 minutes
them away. It's not their fault
ow that when a game is on
relevant.

prepare them in advance.
atch drink though, for it could
ad, prime them the day before
x-a-first-time-fan guide.

Step 1
Put the page opposite
on to a photocopier.

Step 2
Make a few copies.

Step 3
Fill in the details
and fax to your first-
time guest.

FAX-A-FIRST-TIME-FAN™

Dear |_____|

Very pleased you will be coming with us to watch:

(_____) **v** (_____)

on ☐ **Monday** ☐ **Saturday**
☐ **Wednesday** ☐ **Sunday**

We will be meeting in the

|_____| **pub.**

☐ AM ☐ PM

Special directions

DON'T BRING...

- **Bunch of flowers**
- **Tie/blazer**
- **A shooting stick**
- **A bloke you met on the bus/train**

DON'T WEAR...

☐ **Red clothes**
☐ **Blue clothes**
☐ **Orange clothes**
☐ **Green clothes**
☐ **Purple clothes**

DON'T SHOUT...

- **"When do the players break for tea?"**
- **"At least he's keen"**
- **"The other side are a bit tasty aren't they?"**

Disclaimer: Whilst I will make every effort to make this a happy and memorable day, you attend at your own risk. I am not responsible for injury (physical or psychological), food poisoning, weather conditions or disappointment of any kind. I also reserve the right to behave in a surprising and irrational manner at any time during the match. This does not affect your statutory rights in any way.

62:00

FANZINES & PROGRAMMES

What's full of adverts and costs up to £3 a pop?
Yep, the average programme is certainly lacking in the
value-for-money department. And yet thousands of
fans buy one every game.

Who are these people and why do they do it? There
are three types: people who go to games so occasionally
they want a souvenir; misguided loyal fans who think
they owe it to the club to fork out; and anoraks who take
the inky object home unopened and place it in an
immaculate and chronologically ordered collection.

Back in the seventies many hardcore fans tired of the
weekly propaganda puff from the club and looked for
something grittier. They didn't find it so they had to
create it, and the fanzine was born. The first is reputed
to be *Foul*, which was started in 1972 by a group of
Oxford and Cambridge students.

Since then thousands have been produced, some
never making it past issue one, others – like the superb
Sunderland-based *A Love Supreme* (ALS) – turning into
a magnificent publication. But ALS is a rarity because few
fanzines improve by getting slicker. They're normally at
their best when new, raw and outraged – a fog horn blast
to drown out the sound of the club blowing its
own trumpet.

MATHEMATICAL ACROBATICS

While most of us find it hard to recall the shirt numbers of our first team squad, others with more RAM on their mental desktop are capable of computations that astonish and exasperate. These people actually understand the UEFA coefficient for seeding in the Champions' League. And none of them are mathematicians by trade. God invented them simply to torture people like us. They take our strongly held views, prejudices and pet hates and blow them apart with preposterous things, like facts.

But there is something very seductive about stats. They're capable of offering succour in desperate times ('I've worked it out; if we win our last three games 13-0 and they lose all their's by the same margin, we can still stay up'). Or a cheap thrill when the conversation is in danger of veering off football ('Hey, according to this we've headed the ball to the opposition more times than any other team in the Second Division').

Go on, admit you can't help reading those Opta player ratings, even if they did once 'prove' that 39-year-old Dave Beasant was England's obvious choice for national custodian. And how many times have you sat down with a mid-season league table, a fixtures list and a calculator and tried to work out whether you're going to win the league or get relegated? Exactly; you might be rubbish at maths but attempting all sorts of complex calculations is an essential part of being a fan.

$$\text{IF "CITY"}$$
$$w = 3, \quad d = 1$$
$$\text{"LEAGUE POSIT}$$
$$\text{then } x \times (P)$$
$$\left[\underline{or} \quad x \times (P) \right.$$
$$\text{if } w1 =$$

$$so: x \, l$$
$$\therefore 1 - 0 / 2 -$$

(1) Without flood
(2) If no "ENERAL

c & "UNITED" = y

x "GAMES TO PLAY" (P) = $3^{(1)}$

n" (L) = x17 & y16

$w \times 3$ if $y \times (P) = w \times 2 (d \times 1)^{(2)}$

$nst = (w \times 2) + (d \times 1)$

0]

———————————

$(L) 16$ & $y = (L) 17$

$3 - 2 =$ "STAYING UP" (JNST)$^{(3)}$

t failure

EFFECT" is in place.

(3) See the "HOUDINI THEOREM".

FANS ON THE INTERNET

In July 1999 fans logging on to the news section of the official Derby County FC web site got a shock: the team faced a 12-point deduction in the new season because of transfer irregularities. The story whipped round town, the optimists cursing that they'd probably not make a European place now, the pessimists talking of relegation.

They'd needn't have worried. The story was a hoax perpetrated by a particularly smart hacker. 'Basically someone has cracked the code and it's a wind-up,' a club spokesman said, before noting that this was a very serious matter. No doubt the police have been looking for a bloke with a pony tail who lives in the Nottingham area.

A lot of so-called net hooliganism is a lot more straight-forward than that, however. For example, after their team has stuffed someone many net-connected fans go for a quick visit to the chat area on the opposition's site — to offer heartfelt commiseration, of course. There have even been instances of a group of chat users from one club's site attempting to 'take' a rival team's chat room. Yes, the seventies' terrace culture lives on, in a diluted virtual form.

e-hooligans

Attention Soccer Fans! Don't miss this great opportunity to gather around the computer after work and send abusive internet messages to rival fans. "It's jolly good fun," says Charles Gold, 48 (top centre). "Last week I asked someone for a fight and then didn't turn up. Everyone in Corporate Affairs was laughing about that for days."

The Queen, it is said, believes that every town abroad smells of fresh paint since the locals always spruce it up a bit before she arrives. For the fan the experience of other countries is somewhat different. To us the outside world is boarded up and populated by roving camera crews and nuclear-armed police who don't like being called 'mate'.

Foreign travel also teaches you a lot about your fellow fans. The amiable, milk-of-human-kindness types you normally see around you at your home ground have gone. So have the women. And the children. The entire fan base has been boiled down to 25-45 year-old white males wearing shorts. All the vacancies appear to have been occupied by battalions of middle-aged hard nuts, smiling like they're on a school trip. You can spot them easily because they sing songs from the seventies and don't know any of the current team's first names.

You'll keep bumping into small groups of this lot throughout the day. You'll find them pissing up against a statue somewhere in the 'medieval quarter' or arguing with a woman in a doorway near the red light district. You might be the type who enjoys eating tapas by the cathedral while they'll only eat in restaurants that show you pictures of the meals on offer, but don't think you're so very different – you're fans of the same team, there for the same purpose, sitting in the same seats. Like them, you decided to pay a huge amount of money for a one-night, cow-herd of a trip to see your team play in a faraway place simply because you could. Like them, you're public enemy number one the whole time you're there. And like them, you'll find that the whole experience of following your team on foreign soil so good that the result almost (almost) becomes irrelevant.

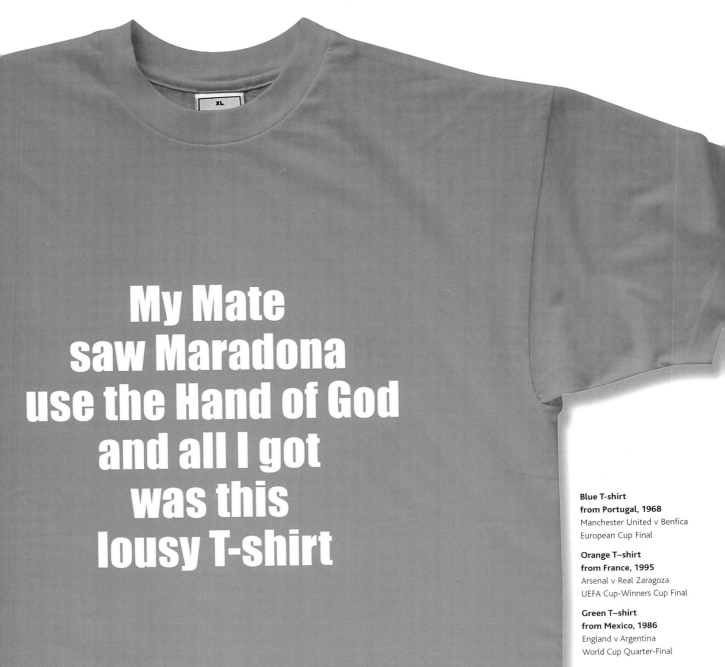

My Mate
saw Maradona
use the Hand of God
and all I got
was this
lousy T-shirt

**Blue T-shirt
from Portugal, 1968**
Manchester United v Benfica
European Cup Final

**Orange T–shirt
from France, 1995**
Arsenal v Real Zaragoza
UEFA Cup-Winners Cup Final

**Green T–shirt
from Mexico, 1986**
England v Argentina
World Cup Quarter-Final

70:00

FANTASY FOOTBALL

Fantasy Football was an imported version of America's obsession with sporting statistics and it sat well with a British public discovering that football could be fun again. Its main effect – aside from turning unlikely lad Frank Skinner into a TV star – has been to make the average supporter far more aware of the attacking potency or defensive qualities of many more footballers than their own. Whereas before many fans didn't give two monkeys who was playing for the opposition, now the stands buzz with in-depth analysis of their right-back's recent performances and points-scoring potential.

The problem is this fantasy stuff can get out of hand. It's all very well cheering on a rival team's number 9 (and your fantasy striker) when you're not playing against them, but it's surely gone too far when you hope they play well against your boys. You may look at the points earned by his last minute equaliser and enjoy your team's Fantasy League position, but deep down you'll still feel dirty.

But it raises all sorts of other questions about your loyalty and your prejudices too. You know that it's probably a good move to have Ginola in your team, for example, but it's not an easy thing to do when you can't stand the sight of him. Head or heart? It's a tough one. The answer is to look at which individuals actually put the most successful fantasy teams together because, for all the agonising you're putting yourself through, most of the leagues seem to be won by someone who got their dog to choose their players.

72:00

TATTOOS

It's the loyalty. Or the sacrifice. Or the, well, defiance of a tattoo. Then again, perhaps it's the bellyful of ale and close proximity of a skin-inker and the impulse. Whatever, many football fans have been struck with the childlike urge to mark their team's colours on to their body. If you must do this, we suggest you follow some of these guidelines. They're not fool-proof, but they might help you avoid years of shame and disappointment.

1. *Avoid dyslexic tattoo 'artists'. The word Rovars, Wunderers or Albino will impress no one. You might like to set a spelling test before the tattoo is begun in earnest.*

2. *Keep it simple. The current version of the club crest is probably too complicated to replicate or, thanks to a flash Herbert who has just joined the marketing department, is probably about to change. If you want a badge then retro is the safest bet, preferably the shirt logo from the sixties or seventies.*

3. *Have the wretched thing applied in your club's town where they know your team colours and crest. There are fewer things sadder than an adult having to explain why their glorious club emblem has turned up on their arm as a splodge. Or why the writing is purple when the team plays in red or blue.*

4. *Consider the ease with which you can conceal this artistic masterpiece. Passing yourself off as a home supporter at an away match may be difficult otherwise. It might, for example, be unwise to walk into the Dolman Stand at Ashton Gate with the word Rovers scrawled across your face.*

5. *Finally, but most important, avoid using players' and managers' names. In an age when club's change personnel quicker than Corinthian Casuals used to change ends, it's important not to expose yourself to sudden transfers or departures. A Blackburn fan with a whim for forwards may, for example, now have a list quite literally as long as their arm saying Garner, Shearer, Sutton, Davies.*

The other thing to ponder as the needle goes in is which of your team's players would be prepared to show their colours in the same way. Apart from Duncan Ferguson and his tattoo declaration of loyalty to Everton, how many other players or managers have backed up their claims that they love the club with a permanent mark? For all the extravagant claims of loyalty you hear uttered at press conferences and in interviews, remember — spoken words come cheaper than those written in ink.

KEEGAN FULHAM AND FOREVER

Loyalty or naivety?
A fan celebrates Kevin Keegan's much-publicised promise to stay at Fulham FC. Keegan accepted the England job a few weeks later.

74:00

ollected by **Zola..**

There's no one moving

He steadies himself   Plays it sideways   ...get's it back...

he looks up...   and still no one is making a run up front.   The noise is

RADIO

Videos fortify some memories at the expense of others. Photos make the mind work harder to build the full picture. TV gets you closest to the real thing. But radio takes you into a new level of anxiety, excitement and emotion completely.

Following your team in audio is a moulding football experience. Back in the days of black-and-white, listeners followed the action from zone to zone, with the pitch divided into sections helpfully supplied in print form in the *Radio Times*. This was the wireless at its most witless.

Now we're more sophisticated, apparently. They tell us that the home team is kicking off towards the goal 'on our right'. Er, surely it might be on our left as we face the radio? How much better to avoid such descriptions and simply form pictures in your fevered mind's eye. You see it all then — how dirty the opposition are and how they've really got 12 men on the pitch, how poor the referee's assistants are, how you woz robbed or what a thing of beauty your passing game is. Ultimately, the joys and the pains of radio are all in the imagination.

Now the front players are beginning to move...

...Oh my word!

The crowd are

they can't believe that one goal might settle it

It's still 0-0, and it's all to play for

...he's clean through

The Wimbledon defe

Wise looks up plays it in fast...

Hughes comes to collect...

brilliant

Zola knocks it short to Wise

He's scored

knocks it wide again to... Sinclair on the over... but there

it's still 0-0

it's in the back

Wimble

Huuuuughess

fantastic

The Wimbledon defence st

deafening inside here Mark H.

Hughes picks it

ughes

they can't belie that

brilliant

That's a

That's a brilliant strik

It's still 0-0 to the

Hughe

...he

Mark Hu

The crowd are going mad

...he's clean through

fantasti

Hughes has scored for C

That's a brilliant strike

a bullet

that went like a rocket

Huuuuughesss!

it's in the bac

The Wimbledon defence stands in a line.

...he's clean through

Huuuuughess

...Oh my word!

Huuuuughesss! a brilliant strike

The crowd are going mad...

fanta

Incredible! ...That's a wonderful goal for The Blues.

76:00

FOOTBALL GAMES

The supporter's desire to fill the gap between matches (or even first and second halves) has spawned a huge industry making games based – according to the manufacturers, at least – on football. Here's a very selective run-down of a few favourites.

Subbuteo

Players swerve on a base that is as wide as they are tall but three or four times heavier. Denied Olympic status in 1992. Spoil-sport rules include no flicking with the thumb. Everyone, by the way, used to break off their diving goalie and glue him back on at a more advantageous angle – not just you.

Striker

The seventies' answer to Subbuteo. You pushed the player on the head and his foot kicked the ball. Opinion divides as to whether this game is a complete classic or absolutely rubbish.

Blow football

What Robbie Fowler did on the pitch after scoring against Everton in 1999, but with the air going in the other direction and, er, straws involved. No meaningful resemblance to football, but popular with cheapskates and parents who knew nothing about sport.

Spot-the-ball

You have to judge where the ball is on a live action photograph. Sounds simple, but it's a well-known fact that each week the position of the ball is decided by a blind-folded chimp holding a felt-tip pen. Do not try to apply the laws of science – just get drunk and guess.

Table/Bar football

Players are fixed in a line on bars and move from side to side (see Arsenal defence for reference), kicking with both feet (similarity to Arsenal defence ends there). Top tip: spinning the players around freestyle really annoys purists.

World Cup Trivial Pursuit

Perhaps most like going to the real thing, i.e. frustrating and makes you swear a lot. If in doubt about an answer, pays to try 'Brazil', 'Billy Bingham' or 'First player to be sent off in a final'.

Computer games

Increasingly life-like mirrors to the real thing. Children mimic the flashy 'plays' performed by virtual stars and some fans look up a prospective foreign signing on 'Championship Manager' before he arrives. PlayStation addicts are easiest to spot – they have glazed expressions and strange divots in the ends of their thumbs.

STRANGER THAN FICTION

Your team may have won, drawn or lost ten on the trot, but it's the unpredictability of the next game that keeps you hooked. Statisticians may be able to 'prove' the likelihood of a result, but every fan knows there are no foregone conclusions in football. But then there's the unexpected and there's the truly bizarre. We're not just talking about nicking a late winner away to the league leaders, we're talking about the Twilight Zone some matches enter, where any form of footballing normality is turned on its head.

Winter 1993, for example, witnessed one of the strangest performances by two international sides. Caribbean rivals Barbados and Grenada faced each other in a cup competition and with just five minutes remaining the home side were leading 2-1.

Normal enough so far. The trouble was they required a win by two clear goals to qualify for the next round, and Grenada's defence was massed in front of their goal. Intriguingly, should the game have gone to penalties the eventual winner would be awarded a two-goal victory under the competition's quirky rules. Recognising the opportunity, the Barbados team resolved to equalise for the opposition and so ensure there was a penalty shoot-out. This they did, with an own goal – 2-2.

Then it gets truly strange. The Grenadans cottoned on to the trick and set off towards their own goal to score the vital 'loser'. And so, to the increasing perplexity of onlookers, the players from Barbados sprang to the defence of their opponents' goal. Against the odds they held out, winning the penalty shoot-out and progressing to the next round.

But weird things can happen anywhere. In 1999 Carlisle United (whose chairman, Michael Knighton, is one of the nation's most fervent UFOlogists) retained their league status when an on-loan player, signed after the transfer deadline under special dispensation from the Football League, scored the winner in the fourth minute of injury time in the very last game of the season. What's more, the scorer – Jimmy Glass – was playing in goal! Of course, in keeping with the strange ways of football, Glass was released from Carlisle the following month.

1966 World Cup Final
Here is England's proudest moment captured in a brilliant image. You've probably seen it many times before, but have you seen the stranger-than-fiction visual accident in it? The photographer has captured it all – the power of Hurst's strike; the furrowed brow of the German defender; Wembley in its finest hour. But he's also created a portrait of a ref who has let this great football moment go to his head.

Stamford Bridge Chelsea FC

Highbury Arsenal FC

Old Trafford Manchester United FC

What was it that inspired Bill to get creative? A passing Inca? A night spent experimenting with Rizlas and his beloved green stuff? Or a new sit-on mower with close-cropping function?

Where will it end? Will the groundsman-artist be adding his signature down by the corner flag? Will the limitations of green lead them to try working in other colours? And what would it be like if a club's pitch patterns said something about them?

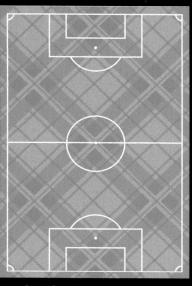

Hampden Park Scotland & Queens Park FC

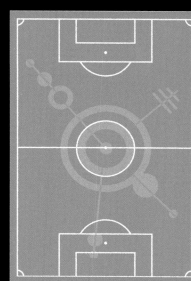

County Ground Swindon Town FC

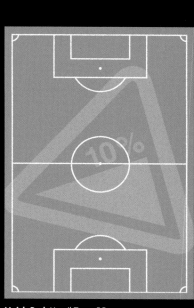

Vitality Park Yeovil Town FC

There are some times when only the best will do. More often than not, though, we fans have to grab anything that's going, and if it has to be the Pedigree Chum Trophy then so be it. The sad truth is that there are only a handful of trophies to be won each season and for the Premiership teams European success is as reliable as a schoolboy goalkeeper, so make the most of the egg cups when they come along. Bring the whole town up to Wembley in a ten-mile fleet of coaches, buy ten copies of that 24-page special in the *Argus* and make sure you celebrate with as much colour and invention as possible.

One of the very finest celebratory traditions is the home made trophy. You see them every final, paraded by proud craftsmen. There are the small ones worn as rosettes, the comic giant ones with big handles and the serious attempts to make one exactly the same dimensions as the real thing (not easy when the original is round and yours is totally flat). It doesn't matter how good it is – you're unlikely to get your hands on the original so any trophy-like construction will do nicely.

People have been making these things for years, but we have Biddy Baxter and Blue Peter to thank for the continuation of this football tradition in modern times. Because of them generations of young fans have grown up able to turn tin foil, an old cardboard box and some glue into a glistening replica. What John Noakes and co. never warned the loyal fan about was what happens when you've been beaten and you have to trudge home carrying a broken heart and a wobbly bit of card and foil. But however bad the humiliation, make sure you get it home in one piece – next year could be your year.

 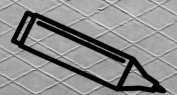 

1: Go down the shops

If you really want an impressive size trophy you will need a stout cardboard box. Some will tell you that a cornflake packet will do just as well, but just wait for a windy match day and watch their flimsy contraptions fold in two. Once you have selected your box, flatten it out and work out how big your cup can be.

2: Draw your dream cup

The professionals would use a bullet-tipped marker to sketch out the shape to be cut, but any old Biro will do so long as you press hard. When drawing your cup try to keep it symmetrical and in proportion. You could try looking in magazines or freeze-frame a cup final you have videoed off the TV.

3: Get a child to help you

Being careful not to scratch your tabletop or poke anyone's eyes out, cut around your outline with a pair of scissors. Take your time and use small snips rather than trying to force the blades. If you have children, it might be best to ask them to do it. They have usually had more practice at this sort of thing.

4: The sticky part

Dab the cardboard cup all over on ONE SIDE only with a proprietary brand of adhesive. Using offcuts from stage 2, spread the glue thinly over the surface. Ensure you have adequate ventilation in the room at this point. DO NOT SMOKE while doing this – ashes in the glue will ruin the effect.

5: The fiddly bit

The potential for disaster at this point is high. You must get the foil on before the glue dries, so it is best to have worked out how many pieces of foil you will need if you are working on a larger cup. N.B. Use only new foil straight off the roll – grease or crumbs will ruin the finished result.

6: Here's one I made earlier

Once you have polished the cup with a soft cloth and allowed the glue to dry, you can then decorate it to your taste. Ribbons, if you can get them, are by far the most effective addition. You are now free to jump up and down, wave your cup in the air and fantasise about lifting the real thing.

INFLATABLES

The fun had gone out of the game in the 1980s. Bad
football. Bad fans. Bradford. Heysel. Hillsborough. Out
of Europe. Falling attendances. A government that hated
football and its fans. A government that banned people
from bringing combs, banners and musical instruments
to grounds. Then, in August 1987, bananas burst forth
from the terraces.

For one reason or another a Man City fan, Frank
Newton, borrowed a five-foot inflatable banana from
a friend and introduced it to the Maine Road terrace.
Over the ensuing weeks it became a cult fruit, soon
joined by more of its kind.

By Christmas City weren't the only fans playfully
indulging themselves. Novelty inflatables of all kinds
appeared. West Ham fans found a source of huge plastic
hammers. Stoke City favoured Pink Panthers. Grimsby
followers adopted a shoal of Harry the Haddock fish.
Wimbledon, meanwhile, made a meal of sausages and
eggs (no, we don't know why either). Other pumped-up
curiosities included toucans, black puddings, parrots,
canaries and gorillas. One afternoon at Maine Road – clearly
the spiritual home of the inflatable – the whole bizarre
activity reached its height when horror heroes Frankenstein
and Godzilla took each other on in an aerated brawl.

Supporters gorged themselves on an innocent bit of
fun for a while, but the air started to escape from the
fad before the season was out. Arsenal, never the most
liberal of clubs, banned the terrace toys in case they
blocked people's view, and the whole craze finally lost
its freshness when inflatable women started to attend
matches with increasing regularity. It begs a question
– what on earth happened to all those air-filled oddities?
Were they all let down gently and left in a bin? Were
they unceremoniously dumped in the gutter? Or are they
sitting in attics all over the land, ready to re-emerge
when football needs to lighten up again?

PAs

There are two kinds of announcements at football grounds: the barely audible phrase with a pinch of static thrown in, or a ton of static with a little bit of indecipherable talking sprinkled on top. Even when you walk down to the front of the stand and stick your ear in direct line with the speaker it still sounds like an asthmatic alien with a heavy lisp trying to communicate using a piece of paper and a comb.

Give it a few years of practice and you can start to work out a bit of what they're trying to say. This, however, is almost always a mistake, for PA announcers also fall into two particularly annoying camps. First, there's the type who end up out there on the pitch because they didn't have enough talent to break into Hospital Radio.

Sure, they've perfected the art of walking round in circles without getting tangled in their microphone lead, but basically they're car-coated smoothies who are a constant source of irritation and embarrassment to the home fans.

The other type of announcer is invisible and far, far more dangerous. This lot are buried somewhere deep within the bowels of the stadium. They've never actually seen a match being played, but they have perfected the knack of making a rambling announcement at a crucial time in a game. Basically, they need to learn that no-one really cares that Jeff's brother Steve is waiting for him by the Bovril Gate; or that Ian Blenkinsop in the East Stand is the proud father of a baby girl. The game is in full flow – normal life can wait.